# CONTENTS

*Gateleg shelf (top left), wall-mounted shelf unit (top right) and glass shelves across window*

# Shelving

Whether you use them for display or storage, shelves make a useful addition to most rooms. The commercial kits and modular systems available may not always be suitable, but the simple designs here can be modified to suit any style or purpose.

*Brackets are the simplest form of shelf support.*

## SHELF SUPPORTS

When deciding on the support for your shelf you need to consider the appearance you want and the weight it will have to hold.

• Shelves are most often supported on brackets of wood or metal. Depending on the spacing of the brackets and the thickness of the shelving material, such shelves can support even heavy weights.

• Shelves can also be supported on a back batten fixed to the wall, or on side battens attached to uprights or the sides of an alcove. Use both for a really strong shelf.

• Bookcases and other shelf units that will support a fair weight are often constructed using housing joints. Butt joints are easier to make, but they will not support as much weight.

• Cantilevered shelves are attractive but cannot support any great weight.

## SHELF SPANS

If you want a shelf of any length, you need to consider the spacing between supports (the span). The table opposite gives a guide to possible spans. There is no hard and fast rule as the span is dependent on the shelf material, the methods used to construct and support it, and the weight you will put on it. Always err on the side of caution: you do not want your shelf to collapse.

## WALL FIXINGS

There are so many building materials and methods used today it can often be difficult to decide on the best method of fixing a shelf to a particular wall. First, find out exactly which methods have been used to build your house and then consult your local hardware supplier. Among the more common fastenings are:

00180753

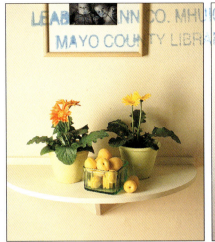

• Plastic wall plug, a hollow plastic tube that expands inside the hole when the right size of screw is inserted. It is suitable for fixing most shelves to masonry walls but not for light-weight concrete, or timber framed walls.

• Plasterboard plug, a cast piece of metal with a coarse thread and self-drilling tip. It is used only for light objects. Once it is inserted in the wall, a screw is placed in its hollow shaft and then screwed tight. Use it in plasterboard and light-weight concrete but not solid masonry.

• Nylon toggle, a toggle with wings that fold back to hold the item securely to the wall. Only suitable for holding light weights, it is used for hollow (plasterboard) walls where no frame member can be found.

• Plastic threaded plug, a hollow plastic plug with coarse thread used for fixing to lightweight concrete blocks. The plug expands when a screw is inserted.

• Spring toggle, a toggle useful for medium weight fixing if no framing member can be found, as long as the wall lining is suitable (plasterboard, timber or plywood).

• Nylon anchor, a device used for medium weight fixing to masonry. It has an expanding nylon sleeve and a nail or screw. Drill a suitably sized hole, insert the anchor in the shelf and align it with the hole. Drive the nail or screw home. The screw is easier to remove than the nail.

• Frame fixers, supplied with own screw and can be inserted through a hole in the complete assembly.

| MAXIMUM SHELF SPANS★ | | |
|---|---|---|
| MATERIAL | THICKNESS | MAXIMUM SPAN |
| Solid timber (PAR) | 19 mm | 750 mm |
| | 32 mm | 1000 mm |
| | 38 mm | 1250 mm |
| Chipboard/MDF | 16–18 mm | 600 mm |
| | 25 mm | 800 mm |
| | 30 mm | 1000 mm |
| Glass | 6 mm | 600 mm |
| | 10 mm | 1000 mm |

★ For shelves supported on brackets at each end with no rear batten. Some sagging may occur if excessive weight is placed on the shelf.

# Shelf fixed with hidden rods

These elegant shelves are fixed to the wall with steel rods and have no visible support. They are strong enough to carry a vase of flowers or a row of pictures but they should not be used for books or for other heavy items or they will sag.

MAKING THE FRAME
1 The shelf is fixed to the wall with steel support rods and their spacing is determined by the type of wall to which you are fixing the shelf. Decide exactly where the shelf is to go and the type of wall.
• For masonry walls the rods should be spaced 450 mm apart: locate one rod in the centre and then measure 450 mm either side to determine the positions of the other rods.

• In plasterboard partition walls studs are usually spaced between 400 mm and 600 mm apart. Locate the stud centres (see the box on page 62). If the studs are at 600 mm centres only two supports can be used. Space them evenly as shown in the diagram on page 9. If studs are positioned at 400 or 450 mm centres, locate the centre rod and then measure out.
• This shelving is not suitable for use with metal frame wall construction.

## MATERIALS FOR TWO SHELVES★

| PART | MATERIAL | LENGTH | NO. |
|---|---|---|---|
| Stiles | 25 x 25 mm pine PAR | 1190 mm | 4 |
| Rails | 25 x 25 mm pine PAR | 243 mm | 10 |
| Lippings (side) | 38 x 25 mm ramin or other hardwood PAR | 300 mm | 4 |
| Lippings (front) | 38 x 25 mm ramin or other hardwood PAR | 1228 mm | 2 |
| Rods | 10 mm (⅜ in) diameter threaded steel rod | 360 mm | 6 |
| Panels | 4 mm plywood | 1200 x 281 mm | 4 |

OTHER: Twelve 10 mm (⅜ in) nuts; PVA adhesive; masking tape; eighteen 40 mm (1½ in) nails; wood filler; abrasive paper: medium; finish of choice

★ Finished width 300 mm, length 1225 mm (see step 1 above if you want to adjust the length). Timber sizes given are nominal (see page 49).

*Hidden steel rods project into the wall to support these neat display shelves.*

## TOOLS

- Tape measure
- Pencil
- Panel saw
- Tenon saw
- Electric drill
- Drill bit: 10 mm
- Solid domestic staple gun
- Old paint brush (optional)
- G-cramps or similar
- Boards for cramping
- Electric router (optional)
- Smoothing plane
- Mitre box or mitre saw
- Hammer
- Nail punch
- Electric sander or cork sanding block
- Spirit level

2 Select your material carefully, choosing timber that is straight and without any twists so that the shelf will remain straight. Cut the stile and rail material to the given lengths. Cut all pieces the same length at once to ensure they correspond exactly.

3 Take the stiles and mark the positions for the steel support rods. Drill holes using the 10 mm drill bit. Also mark where the rails will butt up against the stiles (see the diagram opposite).

4 Butt the rails against the stiles in the positions marked and staple them together. The staples will hold the frame together well enough for you to locate it neatly on the plywood during the gluing process. Make sure the frames are square and will remain that way.

COMPLETING THE SHELF

5 Insert the rods into the holes in the frame, using nuts against the inner sides of the stiles. Make sure the nuts are firm but not tight and the end of the rod is inset approximately 3 mm from the front edge of the frame. The nuts will prevent the shelves being pulled off the rod by accident and will ensure maximum support right across the shelves.

6 Spread a good quantity of adhesive across the bottom of the frame. An

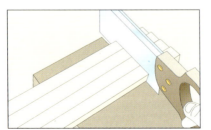

*2 Cut the stile and rail material, cutting all pieces the same length at once so that they correspond exactly.*

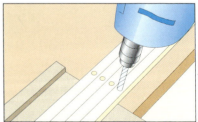

*3 Mark out and drill the holes in the stiles for the steel support rods, using the 10 mm drill bit.*

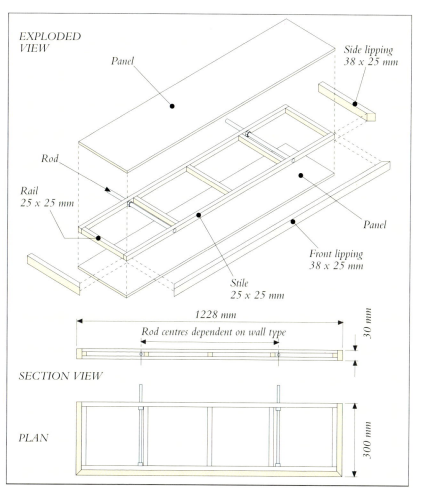

EXPLODED VIEW

Panel

Side lipping
38 x 25 mm

Rod

Rail
25 x 25 mm

Panel

Front lipping
38 x 25 mm

Stile
25 x 25 mm

1228 mm

30 mm

Rod centres dependent on wall type

SECTION VIEW

PLAN

300 mm

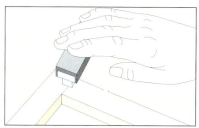

4 Butt the rails against the stiles in the marked positions and then staple them together.

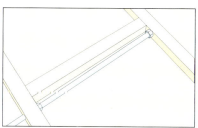

5 Insert the rods into the frame, so that the nuts are firm and the rod is 3 mm in from the front of the frame.

old paint brush will help spread it effectively while keeping your hands clean. Place the frame on the bottom panel. Make sure the back edges of the frame and panel are aligned and use a piece of masking tape to keep them in place—you will not be able to straighten the back edge later as the steel rods will be in the way. The panel should project slightly on all other sides: it will be trimmed after the adhesive has dried.

7 Glue scrap pieces of 25 x 25 mm timber inside the frame area to prevent the panel sinking down between the rails. Spread adhesive on the top of the frame. Lay the top panel on the frame and align the back edge as before. If you are making more than one shelf, place the shelves one on top of the other

with a layer of newspaper between to prevent them sticking together.

8 Place the shelf or shelves on a flat board and place another on top of them to prevent damage when they are cramped and to ensure even distribution of pressure over the plywood and frames. If you have them, use G-cramps or similar cramps, but otherwise stack plenty of weights on top. Check that the frame and panels are perfectly aligned and wipe off any excess adhesive with a damp cloth. Leave to dry overnight.

9 While the adhesive is drying, prepare the edge lippings, which are used to hide the edges of the frames and plywood panels. They also give extra strength to the shelf. Plane the lipping timber to a finished size of 31 x 19 mm and cut the pieces to slightly over length to allow for the mitres: the side lippings have a mitre on one end only and the front lipping has mitres on both ends.

10 Remove the shelf from the cramps and check that the panels

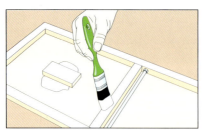

*6 Spread a good quantity of adhesive across the frame and locate the frame on the plywood.*

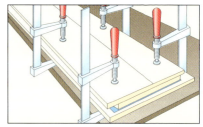

*8 Place flat boards above and below the shelf and apply adjustable cramps or stack plenty of weights on top.*

have stuck successfully to the frame. If not, apply more adhesive and cramp the shelf a second time. If all is well, trim the excess plywood from the frame, using a router with a trimming bit, or clean up the edges with the smoothing plane. Use a smoothing plane to ensure the edges are flat and straight.

11 Hold the front lipping to the front edge of the shelf and mark the inside mitres onto the lipping. Cut the mitres. Apply the two side lippings using two 40 mm (1½ in) nails and a good smear of adhesive. Make sure the mitres are well aligned with the corners of the shelf and the lipping is flush with the top of the shelf (or it can project just over as it can be planed flush later if necessary).

12 Fix the front lipping onto the shelves using five 40 mm (1½ in) nails and some adhesive. If you prefer not to nail on the lippings, they can be attached using long cramps. Do not use tape as this does not give a strong joint and can result in gaps between the lippings and shelves.

13 Use a smoothing plane to flush up the lipping with the top and bottom of the shelf, taking care not to gouge the surface of the plywood. Offsetting the plane blade slightly with the lateral adjustment lever will help prevent gouging. Punch the nail holes and fill any gaps with wood filler. Sand the shelf smooth using medium grade abrasive paper.

## FINISHING AND INSTALLATION

14 Finish the shelf as desired (see the box below).

15 Measure up from the floor to the height where you want the top of the shelf and use a spirit level to strike a level line. Measure down from the line half the thickness of the shelf, line up the support rods with this line and mark the positions.

16 Drill the appropriate number of holes into the wall. Make sure the holes go square into the wall or at a slight downward angle so the shelves are level or slightly pitched up. This will help counteract any sag and stop items falling off the shelf, particularly if your house is subject to vibration from traffic or stomping feet.

### FINISHING YOUR PROJECT

• If painting your shelf, use two coats, sanding between each with fine abrasive paper. Use a primer /undercoat first to fill the timber grain and make it easier to sand. On MDF do not sand the faces too hard as this makes them furry, but work hard on the edges. Use a good quality wood filler to stop up bruises or holes visible before finishing.

• If you intend to use stain or varnish, remove all excess adhesive first or the stain will not penetrate through into the timber and there will be white blotches.

*The dowel rail is an optional feature of this classic slatted shelf.*

# Slatted shelf

This shelf with parallel slats is supported on two end brackets and has a rod fixed from bracket to bracket. It will be useful in the kitchen or in the hallway and can easily be made longer by adding more brackets as necessary.

TOOLS

- Tenon saw
- Smoothing plane
- Square
- Pencil
- Tape measure
- Trimming knife
- Combination square

- Mitre box or mitre saw
- Electric drill
- Drill bits: 5 mm, 3 mm
- Vice
- Cramp
- Hammer

- Cork sanding block (or electric sander)
- Countersink bit
- Screwdriver (slotted or cross-head)
- Spirit level

MATERIALS*

| PART | MATERIAL | LENGTH | NO. |
|---|---|---|---|
| Vertical | 50 x 25 mm pine or other softwood PAR | 300 mm | 2 |
| Horizontal | 50 x 25 mm pine or other softwood PAR | 320 mm | 2 |
| Brace | 50 x 25 mm pine or other softwood PAR | 353 mm | 2 |
| Rod | 12 mm diameter timber dowelling | 600 mm | 1 |
| Slats | 25 x 25 mm pine or other softwood PAR | 680 mm | 11 |

OTHER: PVA adhesive; 40 mm (1½ in) nails; four 50 mm (2 in) x No.10 gauge countersunk brass wood screws; twenty-two 30 mm (1¼ in) x No.8 gauge countersunk brass wood screws; abrasive paper: fine and very fine; wall fixings (see step 15); finish of choice

* Finished width 320 mm, length 640 mm. Timber sizes given are nominal. For timber types and timber sizes, see the box on page 49.

13

## CUTTING OUT

1 Select your material carefully, making certain it is free from twisting and other defects as far as possible. Reduce the materials to the required width and thicknesses by sawing and cleaning up with a smoothing plane. Be sure to remove any machine marks as this will help enhance the final appearance.

2 Mark the required lengths for the vertical and horizontal pieces and use the combination square and pencil to mark the lines all the way around the timbers. Also mark off the lengths on the slats. Use a trimming knife to cut the fibres around the pencil lines before you start sawing, then cut the pieces to the required lengths carefully. Ensure you keep to the waste side of your pencil lines when cutting as timbers can be planed back if necessary but not lengthened.

3 Using the combination square, mark out and cut the brace pieces. The longest edge is to the outside and is 353 mm long.

4 Mark out the centres of the braces pieces where the dowels will be inserted. Drill the holes for the dowels, using the correct size bit, to a depth of 10 mm.

5 Trim all the components to their exact lengths. Place the common components together in the vice and plane the end grain back to the marking knife lines. To help prevent the end grain breaking out, use a backing block of the same material located just a millimetre or so below the marking knife lines. Remember that your plane needs to be razor sharp and set quite fine to achieve a good result.

6 Cramp all the slats together with the ends flush and plane the chamfer across one edge of all the ends at the same time. Turn them over and repeat the process until all the ends have been chamfered all round. One end of the vertical and horizontal pieces can be chamfered similarly, but only on the short sides and one long side.

*1 Plane the materials to the required width and thicknesses and clean up with a smoothing plane.*

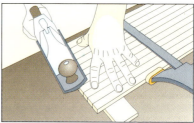

*6 Cramp all the slats together with the ends flush and plane the chamfer across all pieces at the same time.*

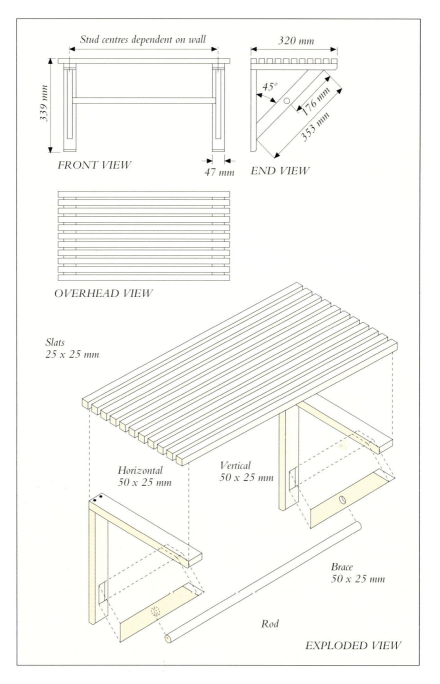

Stud centres dependent on wall

339 mm

FRONT VIEW

47 mm

320 mm

45°

176 mm

353 mm

END VIEW

OVERHEAD VIEW

Slats
25 x 25 mm

Horizontal
50 x 25 mm

Vertical
50 x 25 mm

Brace
50 x 25 mm

Rod

EXPLODED VIEW

*Slatted shelves are traditionally used in the kitchen, bathroom or hallway.*

### ASSEMBLY

7 Sand all the components. If you are going to stain the shelf it is a good idea to stain the components now as some places will be difficult to get at once the shelf is assembled.

8 Glue and nail the vertical and horizontal pieces together using 40 mm (1½ in) nails so the chamfered ends are at the bottom of the verticals and the front of the horizontals.

9 Locate the braces on the brackets as shown in the diagram and mark the inside and outside positions of the joints on both verticals and horizontals. Mark the centre line of the joints and measure from the inside of the brace joint 15 mm along the centre line to locate the position for the screw fastening. Drill 5 mm holes and countersink for the screws on the external faces. Align the braces in the brackets and screw and glue them into position using the 50 mm (2 in) x No.10 gauge screws.

10 Check the wall to determine the type of construction used as this will affect the spacing of the brackets. For masonry construction, space the brackets at 600 mm centres; for timber frame construction the positions will be determined by the spacing of the studs (usually somewhere between 400 mm and 600 mm). To find the studs, use one of the methods in the box on page 62. Having determined the positions of the brackets, make any necessary adjustment to the length of the rod.

11 Cramp all the slats together and mark out the bracket distances evenly

*8 Glue and nail the vertical and horizontal pieces together, using the 40 mm (1½ in) nails.*

*9 Locate the braces on the brackets and mark the inside and outside positions of the joints.*

across all slats. Mark off a line slightly to one side of the centre line so that the slat screws will not interfere with the brace fixing screws. Drill 5 mm holes in each slat and countersink them for neatness.

12 Start fixing the slats by aligning the first one with the front edge of one bracket. Slip in the rod, bring in the next bracket and fasten the slat to it with a 30 mm (1¼ in) x No.8 gauge screw. Next, use an 8 mm spacer to position the next slat and each subsequent slat. Ensure that the brackets remain square to the slats and that the slat ends are lined up.

## FINISHING AND INSTALLATION

13 The shelf will require a minimum of two coats of whichever finish you have chosen, either varnish over the stain already applied or paint. A brush will do the job but it will be very difficult to reach some places and so it is recommended that you use a spray can. A final preparatory sand with fine grade abrasive paper will be okay, but use very fine paper between coats. See the box on page 11 for finishing tips.

---

HINT

Always make sure your cutting tools are very sharp before you begin work. Sharp tools will not only make work easier, they will allow you to make the cuts much more precisely.

---

14 Drill two 5 mm holes in each bracket for fixing. They will be less noticeable on the inside of the brace. Do not forget to countersink them.

15 Position the shelf on the wall and drill a pilot hole into the wall. The size will depend on the fastening you use and the wall construction. For masonry walls you should use 75 mm (3 in) nylon anchors, 75 mm (3 in) x No.10 gauge countersunk screws with plastic wall plugs or 75 mm (3 in) countersunk frame fixers. For framed walls, 75 mm (3 in) x No.10 gauge countersunk wood screws should be used. Fix in one fastening first, then bring the shelf to the level position, checking with a spirit level. Drill the wall and fix the second fastening. Test that the shelf is level and make any adjustments before securing it with the final fastenings.

*Braced brackets are used to firmly fix the shelf to the wall.*

# Shelf with lip

This simple shelf is perfect for displaying plates or other small items and yet it is very easy to make. The shelf itself rests on a back batten and the lip attached to the front of it prevents the objects slipping forward.

| MATERIALS★ | | | |
|---|---|---|---|
| PART | MATERIAL | LENGTH | NO. |
| Wall support | 100 x 19 mm pine PAR | 1500 mm | 1 |
| Shelf | 75 x 25 mm pine PAR | 1500 mm | 1 |
| Lip | 50 x 25 mm pine PAR | 1500 mm | 1 |

OTHER: Twenty 40 mm (1½ in) x No.8 gauge screws; PVA adhesive; water-based wood filler; abrasive paper: one sheet of medium and two sheets of fine; wallplugs (if mounting on masonry wall); finish of choice

★ Finished width behind lip 77 mm; length 1500 mm. The length can be adjusted to suit your location. Timber sizes given are nominal. For timber types and timber sizes, see the note on page 49.

*The lip on this shelf projects upward just enough to hold a plate or picture frame in place. It will not obscure your view of them.*

## MAKING THE SHELF

1 Using the straight slots of a mitre box to keep the saw square, cut all three pieces of timber to exactly 1500 mm long (or desired length).

2 Take the wall support and the lip, and mark on the face of the timber the positions for the screws that will attach them to the shelf (see the diagram on page 21). On the wall support, mark positions 10 mm down from the top edge. Place them 50 mm in from each end and approximately 200 mm apart. On the lip, mark positions 15 mm down from the top edge, 50 mm from each end and 200 mm apart. Using the

| TOOLS | | |
|---|---|---|
| • Mitre box | • Drill bits: 5 mm, 3 mm | • Cork sanding block |
| • Tenon saw | • Countersink | • Spirit level |
| • Pencil | • Screwdriver (or screwdriver bit for drill) | (If fixing to a masonry wall, you will need an electric hammer drill and masonry drill bit to suit) |
| • Tape measure |  |  |
| • Fold-out rule | • Filling knife |  |
| • Electric drill |  |  |

*The lip is attached to the shelf so that it projects both above and below.*

5 mm drill bit, drill holes through each piece of timber on the marks and countersink the holes so the screw heads will be just below the surface.

3 Using the medium grade abrasive paper wrapped around the cork block, sand all the timber, removing any pencil marks and blemishes. Dust off.

4 Lay the shelf piece front edge down on the workbench and position the wall support flush with the top edge of the shelf. Placing a nail through the holes in the support, mark the screw positions onto the

shelf. Remove the wall support. Using the 3 mm drill bit, drill holes on the marks to about 30 mm deep. Wipe clean, and apply adhesive along the edge. Reposition the wall support, and then screw the shelf and support together. Wipe off any excess adhesive with a damp cloth.

5 Turn the shelf over so the support is lying on the bench. Repeat to attach the lip to the shelf, positioning the lip so its top is 6 mm higher than the shelf (see the diagram opposite).

6 Fill the screw holes in the lip with wood filler. When it is dry, sand the surface with medium abrasive paper around a sanding block. Change to fine paper and sand the whole piece.

7 Dust off well and apply the desired finish (see the box on page 11).

FIXING IN POSITION
8 Drill holes in the wall support, as close to the underside of the shelf as possible. The spacing of the holes and the method of drilling will be determined by your wall. If you have

*2 On the lip mark the positions for the screws that will hold it to the shelf. Drill the holes.*

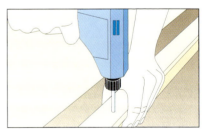

*5 Attach the lip to the shelf, positioning it so that it projects 6 mm above the shelf.*

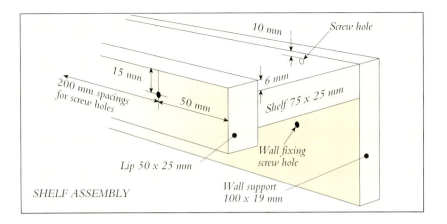

10 mm

Screw hole

15 mm

200 mm spacings
for screw holes

6 mm

50 mm

Shelf 75 x 25 mm

Wall fixing
screw hole

Lip 50 x 25 mm

SHELF ASSEMBLY

Wall support
100 x 19 mm

a masonry wall, space the holes 400 mm apart. On a stud partition wall (usually a plasterboard surface), find the timber studs to drill into—they will be 400–600 mm apart (see the box on page 62). Once you have found the studs, measure and mark the corresponding positions onto the support, close to the underside of the shelf. Drill holes on the marks, using the 5 mm drill bit and countersink the holes so the screw heads will be below the surface.

9 Hold the shelf in position (you may need help) and sit the spirit level on the shelf. Using a nail (or the drill and 3 mm drill bit), mark the wall through the holes. Remove the shelf. For a masonry wall, use a masonry drill bit suitable for the size of the wall plug and drill holes 40 mm deep. Insert plastic plugs into the holes. For a stud partition wall, use the 3 mm drill bit and drill holes about 30 mm deep on the marks. Screw the shelf in place, driving the screw heads below the support surface.

10 Fill in over the screw heads with wood filler and allow it to dry. Sand lightly and touch up the finish.

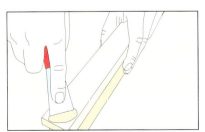

*6 Fill the countersunk screw holes with wood filler to make an even surface ready for finishing.*

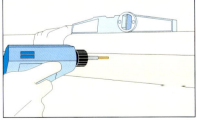

*9 Use a spirit level to ensure the shelf is level and mark the wall through the holes in the support.*

# Small box shelf

This simple backless box will have many uses around the home. It consists of a top and bottom, two ends and a rail for fixing to the wall. This shelf is easy to make, using simple tools and traditional technology.

## CUTTING OUT

1 Mark out the required lengths on the timber, leaving 5 mm between each part for the saw cut and for cleaning back. Use the square to square the lines across the face and around all sides of the timber. Check that the lines are square and when you are satisfied retrace the lines using a trimming knife to cut the top fibres. This reduces the breaking out of fibres on the under side of the cut and reduces the need for filler at a later stage.

| MATERIALS★ | | | |
|---|---|---|---|
| PART | MATERIAL | LENGTH | NO. |
| End | 150 x 25 mm solid timber PAR | 148 mm | 2 |
| Top/bottom | 150 x 25 mm solid timber PAR | 240 mm | 2 |
| Rail | 50 x 25 mm solid timber PAR | 240 mm | 1 |

OTHER: Twelve 40 mm (1½ in) nails; PVA adhesive; wood filler; two 50 mm (2 in) x No.8 gauge countersunk screws, solid wall plugs or hollow wall anchors

★ Finished height 148 mm; length 284 mm; width 140 mm. Timber sizes given are nominal. For timber types and sizes, see page 49.

| TOOLS | |
|---|---|
| • Pencil | • Hammer |
| • Tape measure | • Nail punch |
| • Carpenter's square | • Electric drill (for installation) |
| • Trimming knife | • Drill bit: 5 mm (for installation) |
| • Hand saw or circular saw | • Screwdriver (slotted or cross-head) |
| • Vice | • Spirit level |
| • Plane | |

*This simple box shelf is perfect for spare rolls of toilet paper, but remember not all rolls are the same size. You may need to adjust the dimensions of the box.*

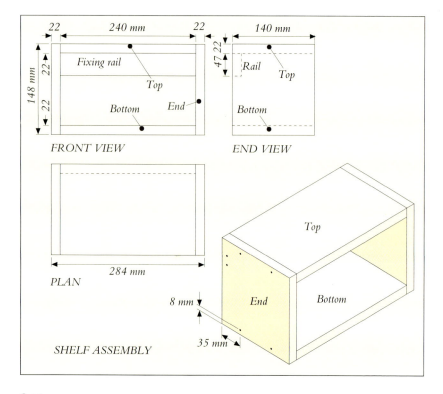

FRONT VIEW

END VIEW

PLAN

SHELF ASSEMBLY

2 If you are using a circular saw, use a straight timber batten to run your saw against to ensure a square cut. Cut the components to length.

3 Take the parts of the same size and hold them together in the vice. Ensure the marking knife lines are aligned. With a fine set on the plane, plane the ends down to the correct length. To do this, plane towards the centre from each side of the parts so as to prevent the timber chipping (this happens when you have too much blade sticking out of the bottom of the plane and continually plane past the end of the material).

Check that you have planed each part to a peak in the centre and that you are planing square to the face of the material. Then work from the centre towards the outside edges to plane the peak down flat. Regularly check that each part is square. Repeat this step for each part of the job, including the fixing rail.

ASSEMBLY
4 Take the top and place it in the vice, end up. Take one end and determine the outside and front and top edges. On the outside, about 10 mm down from the top edge and 35 mm in from the front and back

## TIMBER OR MDF?

If you need to buy timber to make this project, it will be cheaper to buy the solid timber specified, but there is no reason why you cannot make this project from 18 mm MDF if you have a piece of the required size in your workshop or if your local joinery shop will sell you an offcut.

edges, start a 40 mm (1½ in) nail. Spread adhesive on the edge to be joined, use your finger to spread the adhesive and rub it well in. Apply a second thin coat of adhesive to the joint and bring the two parts together. Nail the joint together. Try and keep the face and edges flush.

5 Following the same method, join the bottom to the end. Turn the box over and nail on the other end.

6 Insert the fixing rail and nail it home. Punch the nail heads below the surface and fill the holes.

## FINISHING AND INSTALLATION

7 Finish the shelf as desired (see the box on page 11).

8 Decide where the shelf should be fixed. It will be fastened to the wall through the fixing rail and placing a little construction adhesive on the rail before final fixing will help secure the unit to the wall, but if you

ever want to move the unit the adhesive bond will be hard to break and any excess will be hard to remove from the walls.

• If you are fixing the shelf to a masonry wall, drill two 5 mm holes in the fixing rail about 180 mm apart and 30 mm down from the top edge. Position the unit on the wall, using a spirit level to make sure it is horizontal, and mark the position for drilling on the wall. Use a masonry bit suitable for the size of the wall plug being employed to drill the holes in the wall, place the wall plugs in the holes and screw the unit into position.

• If your walls are not solid masonry, use hollow wall anchors to fix the shelf in position, following the manufacturer's instructions and using a spirit level to be sure it is positioned horizontally.

## MDF

MDF means medium density fibreboard. It is an ideal material for building furniture as you can use a plane and router on it and it does not need to have a finish added, although it will take paint or varnish if desired.

However, MDF does contain chemicals that can cause skin problems in some people. When handling it, wear gloves if you have sensitive skin and always protect your eyes, nose, mouth and lungs from dust.

# Small display shelves

These small display shelves consist of two parts. The narrow back part is fixed to the wall and the main section is then fixed on to it by tightly fitting dowels, so that the wall fixings are completely hidden. Only light items should be placed on these shelves.

METHOD

1 Take the sheet of MDF and lay it on the bench. Make sure one long edge is straight and square. Set the combination square to 152 mm and using your pencil and square mark out a strip of material 152 mm wide. Cramp a straight edge to the sheet to guide the power saw and cramp the sheet of material to a suitable surface for sawing, one that is stable. Be sure that the path the saw will travel is clear of any obstacles, particularly electric flexes. Check that the blade will cut on the waste side of the line.

Cut off the strip, repeating the process until you have enough 150 mm wide strips for your shelves.

2 Using your tape measure or fold-out rule, mark off on the strips (or the length of timber) the length of each of the shelves. We made five shelves 180 mm, 230 mm, 280 mm, 330 mm and 380 mm long. Square these marks across the face of the material, over the edges and back across the bottom face with a combination square and pencil. Go back over the lines with a trimming

---

MATERIALS★

• 1200 x 600 mm sheet of 18 mm MDF or 1500 mm of 150 x 25 mm planed timber

• Fifteen 8 mm diameter timber dowels

• Ten 50 mm (2 in) spring toggles (for hollow wall fixing) or ten 50 mm (2 in) x No.8 gauge screws and wall plugs (for masonry walls)

• Construction adhesive (optional)

• PVA wood adhesive

★ Finished width 150 mm; lengths 180–380 mm. For a note on MDF see the box on page 25. For timber types and sizes see page 49.

---

TOOLS

• Pencil

• Combination square

• Trimming knife or marking knife

• Hand saw or circular saw

• Plane

• Tape measure or folding rule

• Cramp

• Electric drill

• Drill bits: 8 mm, 5 mm

• Countersink bit

• Spirit level

*Each of these elegant little shelves is 150 mm wide but the length varies.*

knife and combination square to cut the top layer of fibres. This prevents the fibres breaking out and gives a crisp edge to the saw cuts.

3 Cut the shelves to length. Lightly plane the edges and ends to remove any saw marks you may have left. If you want to run a fancy moulding around the edges, do it now.

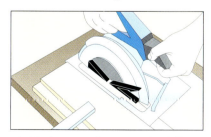

*1 Mark out and cut a strip 150 mm wide. If using a circular saw, cramp a straight edge to the sheet to guide it.*

4 Cramp all the shelves together so the ends are flush at one end and the back edges are uppermost. Mark in from the end 30 mm for the dowel holes and a further 15 mm for the wall fixing holes. (The number of wall fixing points varies according to the length of the shelves. Shelves 100–450 mm long require two fastenings, those 450–600 mm require three and those 600–900 mm long four.) Square a line across the edges with your square and pencil. Remove the cramp, flush up the opposite ends and replace the cramp. Repeat the marking process. Now mark the centre of each shelf on the edge and square a line across the centre of each for the centre dowel hole. Use a marking gauge or the combination square to find the centre in thickness of the shelving material and mark out the centres for the dowel holes and the fixing holes.

5 Cramp the shelves together in a vice or cramp (see the illustration on page 29) and drill the dowel holes using an 8 mm dowelling bit. Drill the holes 45 mm deep (see Hint on page 29). Only drill the dowel holes at this stage.

6 Set the combination square to 20 mm and mark a line this distance from the back edge of one shelf. Place a cross or mark across this line on the upper face to indicate the joint edges. Using the method described in step 1, set up a straight edge on the shelf and use the saw to cut along the 20 mm line. Repeat on the other shelves. Each shelf should

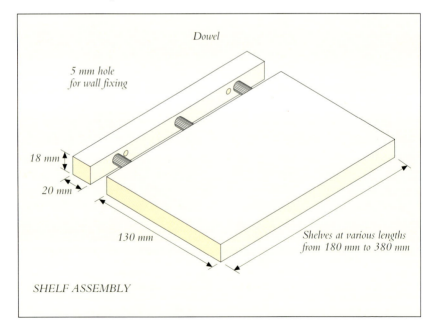

*Dowel*

*5 mm hole for wall fixing*

*18 mm*

*20 mm*

*130 mm*

*Shelves at various lengths from 180 mm to 380 mm*

*SHELF ASSEMBLY*

now be in two parts, one 130 mm wide and one 20 mm wide. Insert the dowels and dry fit the two parts together. They should fit perfectly. This joint is the basis of the hidden fixing method.

7 Take the narrow pieces and drill 5 mm holes for the wall fixings, at the positions marked out in step 4 (45 mm in from the ends and in the centre of the edge). Countersink the fixing holes on the inside joint so that the screw heads will not hold the joint apart. Check that the joint closes flush.

## FINISHING AND INSTALLATION

8 Finish the shelves as desired (see the box on page 11).

9 Choose the location for each shelf very carefully because you will not be able to move these shelves without having to patch the walls afterwards. Use a spirit level to mark a level line on the wall. On the line mark out the distance corresponding to the fastening holes in the shelf and

---

HINT

Wrap a piece of masking tape around the drill bit at the required depth to act as a guide when you are drilling holes to a specified depth.

---

drill holes for the appropriate fasteners, before fixing the narrow part of the shelf to the wall. Placing a small bead of construction adhesive along the line will improve the holding power, particularly if hollow wall anchors are used.

10 Place a small amount of PVA adhesive in each dowel hole and spread a small bead of it along the edges joining the two pieces. Insert the dowels into their holes and push the two parts of the shelf together. Check that the joints have closed up neatly and that all the faces and edges are flush. Wipe off any excess adhesive with a wet cloth and leave the shelves to dry for at least twenty-four hours before placing anything on them.

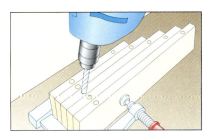

*5 Cramp the shelves together and drill the holes for the dowels that will hold the shelves together.*

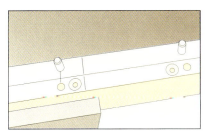

*7 Countersink the holes on the inner face so that the fastenings do not hold the two parts of the shelf apart.*

*The glass shelf was purchased cut to size and with polished edges for safety.*

# Cantilevered glass shelf

Brilliantly simple in concept, this glass shelf cantilevered from a timber rail is very easy to make. It will look equally at home as a display shelf in the living room or in the bathroom.

MAKING THE RAIL

1 Use a rule to mark out the length on the timber. Square the lines all around with the combination square; score them with a knife and square to prevent the fibres breaking out.

Cut the timber to length, making sure you keep to the waste side of the line and that the cut is square.

2 Mark out the position of the groove and bevels on one end of the

## MATERIALS★

- 600 mm length of 100 x 50 mm planed timber

- 600 x 120 mm piece of 6 mm thick glass (see box on page 41)

- Abrasive paper: fine

- Two 38 mm (1½ in) x No.6 gauge countersunk screws

- Clear silicone sealant

★ Finished length 600 mm; width 130 mm. Timber sizes given are nominal (see the box on page 49).

length; double check to see that the marking out is accurate. Use a combination square to transfer the groove marks along the face of the timber to the opposite end of the material, and then set out the groove and bevels again on the other end.

3 Set up the fences on the saw bench or router for cutting the groove. Check that the depth of cut is going to be accurate. Use an offcut or scrap piece of material to check the adjustments before you make any cuts in the good piece. Put on your

safety goggles, hearing protection and dust mask. Now make the first cut. Keep your fingers away from the blade and use a push stick to hold and push the timber through the last part of the cut. Because a saw blade is narrower than the width of the groove required, adjust the fence for the second cut. Use the same piece of scrap wood to check your adjustments and check that a 6 mm

## TOOLS

- Tape measure or fold-out rule
- Pencil
- Combination square
- Trimming or marking knife
- Circular saw bench★
- Safety goggles
- Ear protectors
- Dust mask
- Vice
- Plane
- Electric drill
- Drill bit: 5 mm
- Cork sanding block
- Screwdriver (cross-head or slotted)
- Sealant gun

★ Optional. If you do not have a circular saw bench, you can achieve the same results using a circular saw, set up under a bench in a similar way using fences and stops to cut the groove and bevel the faces.
  Alternatively, a router can be used to cut the groove and a hand plane to bevel the faces. See the box on page 32 if you are using these alternative tools.

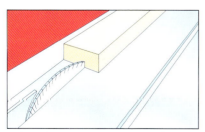

*3 Cut the groove using a circular saw bench (as here) or router. Keep your fingers well clear of the blade.*

SHELVING

PLANING THE BEVELS

Mark the planing angles on the end of the timber. Place the timber in a vice or cramp it down so that you can plane the angle on one edge. At first have enough blade out to take a fair amount off in one pass. Check the angle regularly. As planing becomes more difficult, reduce the amount of blade exposed. Turn the piece around and plane the bevel on the opposite edge.

piece of glass will fit in the groove. The glass should fit neatly in the groove, not too tightly and not loosely at all. Run the second cut. Finally, check that the groove is clean and the glass fits neatly.

4 Make sure the saw blade has completely stopped before you tilt the saw over to 45 degrees. Cut the wider bevel first. Adjust the fence on the saw to 40 mm, and check the set-up by holding the timber up to the blade. Make the first bevel cut.

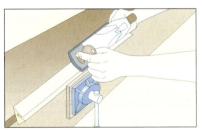

*5 Place the bevelled rail in a vice and carefully plane the edges to remove the saw marks.*

Now set up for the second bevel cut the same way, but reduce the depth of the cut so that the blade cuts into only one side of the groove. When you are satisfied with the set-up, cut the second bevel.

5 Place the bevelled rail into a vice, being careful not to damage the edges, and plane the bevelled faces to remove any saw marks.

FINISHING AND INSTALLATION

6 Decide where the shelf is to go and determine the type of wall construction used. If it is a timber stud wall, determine the distance between the stud centres and transfer the dimension to the back of the rail. The markings should be in line with the groove, as the fastenings will be placed in the groove. At these positions drill 5 mm holes through the support and check that the heads of the fastenings fit into the groove. If not, the heads may be filed down slightly to fit.

7 Using the sanding block and fine grade abrasive paper, sand the bevels smooth. Finish the shelf as desired (see box on page 11), but consider where you will put it. It could go in a bathroom or even a shower recess, but then all surfaces would need to be sealed with paint or varnish (which will reduce the width of the groove).

8 Using a spirit level at the height required, draw a level line on the

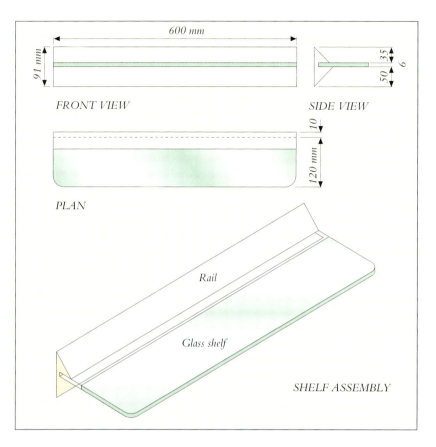

600 mm

91 mm

FRONT VIEW

35
6
50

SIDE VIEW

10

120 mm

PLAN

Rail

Glass shelf

SHELF ASSEMBLY

wall. Hold the rail up to the line and place a nail in the fixing holes to mark the position for the pilot holes. If the wall is difficult to mark with a nail, transfer the marks with a pencil and rule. Drill the appropriate size of hole, insert the fastenings and screw the rail to the wall.

9 Place the shelf in the groove and mark on the shelf the depth that it penetrates the support. Remove the shelf and place masking tape on the outside of these marks. Also mask

around the groove. This will make it easier to remove excess silicone. Now place a fine bead of clear silicone sealant in the groove and push the shelf into the groove, adjusting the fit. Immediately remove any excess silicone sealant with your finger, taking care not to spread it on other areas. Then remove all the tape before the silicone has a chance to set.

10 Leave the shelf for twenty-four hours to allow the silicone sealant to dry before placing anything on it.

# Wall-mounted shelf unit

A small unit of open shelves can hold spices and other kitchen items, a collection of miniatures or even rows of tiny plants.

| MATERIALS★ | | | | |
|---|---|---|---|---|
| PART | MATERIAL | LENGTH | WIDTH | NO. |
| End | 12 mm MDF | 490 mm | 115 mm | 2 |
| Top/bottom | 12 mm MDF | 400 mm | 115 mm | 2 |
| Shelves | 12 mm MDF | 384 mm | 115 mm | 2 |

OTHER: One packet 30 mm (1¼ in) panel pins; PVA adhesive; wood filler; wall fixings; finish of choice

★ Finished height of unit 498 mm; width 400 mm; depth of shelves 115 mm. For a note on MDF, see the box on page 25.

## CUTTING COMPONENTS

1 Cramp the MDF to a portable workbench. Cramp a batten to the board to guide the saw along the cut. Cut three 118 mm wide strips.

2 Hold the strips together in the portable workbench so that the edges are flush. Plane the edges so that they are straight and free from cut marks.

Remove them from the workbench and use the combination square (set it at 115 mm) to mark the finished width of the strips along the face. Do not mark near the edge you have just planed. Bring all three strips together again with their planed edges flush and put them back in the portable workbench or vice and plane the strips together down to 115 mm.

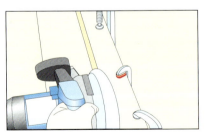

*1 Cramp the MDF to a portable workbench and cramp a batten to the board to guide the saw.*

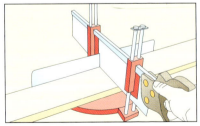

*3 Cut the components to length using a tenon saw. A mitre saw will help keep the cuts square.*

*Housing joints hold the shelves on this simple unit. It has no back, and the wall behind can be painted the same colour as the rest of the wall to emphasise this, or it can be painted to match the shelves.*

3 Using the rule, pencil and square, set out the length of the components along the three strips, leaving 3–5 mm between each part to allow for saw cuts. Mark the pencil lines on all sides of the material. Trace along the lines with a trimming knife to cut the top fibres. Use the tenon saw to cut all parts to the marked length.

4 Take the matching parts and hold them together in a vice, making sure the marking knife lines match up. Use the smoothing plane to square

## TOOLS

- Straight-edge
- Circular saw
- Vice or portable workbench
- Plane
- Combination square
- Pencil
- Trimming knife
- Tenon saw or mitre saw
- Electric router
- 12 mm straight cutting bit or smaller
- Hammer
- Nail punch
- Filling knife

up the ends of the parts and to bring them to the correct lengths. Repeat this process for all the pairs of parts.

5 Using a pencil and combination square, mark out the positions for the rebates on the top and bottom pieces. They will be 12 mm wide and 8 mm deep. Make sure they are in the bottom of the top piece and the top of the bottom piece. Then mark out the housings for the shelves on the inside face of the side pieces. To do this measure up 162 mm from the end of the piece and draw a line across. Then measure up 12 mm for the top of the housing. The second housing is 150 mm further up. The housings are 4 mm deep.

6 The rebates can be cut with the tenon saw and a chisel but are more easily made with a router. Set the router cutter to a depth of 8 mm and the fence to about 8 mm for the width of the cut. Make the first pass over the cutter with a scrap piece of material and make any adjustments to the depth of the cut at this time. Cut the rebates in the top and bottom pieces. Adjust the fence for the second pass of the material over the cutter to the full width of the cut at 12 mm. Be sure to make a test cut on a scrap piece of material first. Finally, check to see that the rebates will fit neatly.

7 For the housing cuts, set the fence 158 mm away from the closest cutting edge of the router cutter and reduce the depth of cut to 4 mm. Make a test cut in a scrap of material. If you are using a full 12 mm cutter check the fit of the material in the housing joint. When satisfied with the depth and position of the housing make the cuts in the side pieces. Work from each end as the spacings are equal. If the cutter is smaller than 12 mm, adjust the fence to make the groove 12 mm wide. Use a test piece to check your adjustments, and then cut the housing joints.

ASSEMBLY
8 Test that all the parts fit together accurately; make any adjustments. When you are satisfied, pull the components apart and apply adhesive to the housing joints. Assemble the joints and join them together using 30 mm (1¼ in) panel pins. Apply adhesive to both faces of the rebate

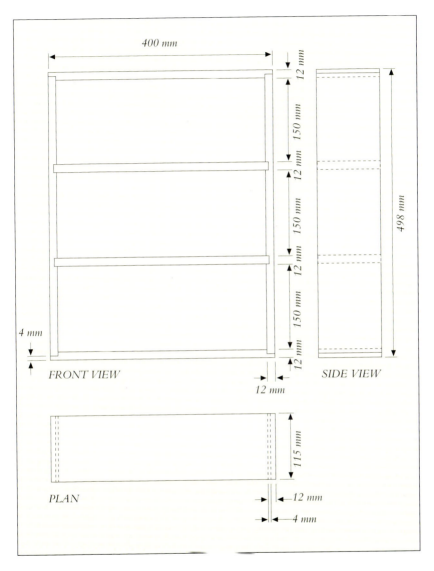

400 mm

12 mm

150 mm

12 mm

150 mm

12 mm

150 mm

12 mm

498 mm

4 mm

FRONT VIEW

12 mm

SIDE VIEW

115 mm

PLAN

12 mm

4 mm

joints; bring together with the rest of the unit. Nail together through the sides with 30 mm (1¼ in) panel pins.

9 Punch and fill all the nail holes and rub back the filler when it has dried.

Apply the finish of your choice (see the box on page 11).

10 Fix to the wall with mirror plates, screws and hollow wall anchors or small wall plugs.

*Glass shelves turn this window into a mini conservatory. It is an ideal use of the centre panel, which does not open.*

# Glass shelves across window

These glass shelves are fitted into timber brackets, which can be fixed across a window or any alcove. The length of the shelves can be varied to fit, but you will need to adjust the glass thickness and the width of the brackets accordingly.

## MAKING THE BRACKETS

1 Make a cardboard template for the bracket, using the diagram on page 40 as a guide but adjusting it to fit your situation. In particular, the width of the bracket should be at least one-third the depth of the shelf, and it should be even wider if heavy items are to be placed on the shelf. If necessary the brackets can protrude beyond the reveal and architrave. Use the pair of compasses to form the curved section but do not make the curve too tight or you will have difficulty manoeuvring the jigsaw around it. Take a pair of scissors and cut out the template.

2 Using the template, mark out the bracket shape on the timber. Remember the brackets will be in pairs, so turn the template over and mark out the reverse pattern. Repeat for as many shelves as you are making. Leave 3 mm between each bracket as an allowance for saw cuts.

---

### MATERIALS★

- Cardboard
- 25 mm thick planed timber (50 mm, 75 mm, 100 mm or 125 mm wide)
- Glass for shelves (see page 41)
- Masking tape
- Abrasive paper: one sheet each of medium and fine
- Six 40 mm (1½ in) panel pins or screws and wall plugs
- Paintable silicone

★ For three shelves. For timber types and sizes, see page 49.

---

### TOOLS

- Pencil
- Compasses
- Scissors
- Tape measure
- Combination square

- Craft knife or scalpel
- G-cramp
- Tenon saw
- Hammer or mallet
- 6 mm chisel (bevel edge or mortise type)

- Jigsaw or coping saw
- Vice
- Smoothing plane
- Cork sanding block
- Spirit level

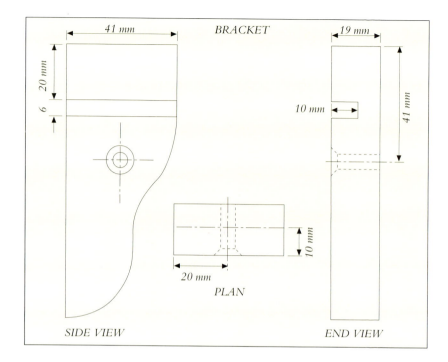

BRACKET

41 mm

20 mm

6

SIDE VIEW

19 mm

41 mm

10 mm

20 mm

10 mm

PLAN

END VIEW

Place an 'x' on the face of each bracket near what will be the top to guide you as you mark them out.

3 From the top of each bracket mark down a distance of 20 mm to establish the top of the groove for the glass shelf. From this mark square a line across the face and down each edge a distance of 10 mm (the depth of the groove). From this last line, mark off the thickness of the glass shelf you intend to use (either 6 mm, 10 mm or 12 mm). Square the line across the face and down each edge a distance of 10 mm.

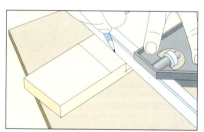

*2 Use the cardboard template to mark out the bracket shape on the timber, reversing it for the opposite face.*

*3 Mark the position of the groove, squaring the line across the face and down the edge to a depth of 10 mm.*

4 Using a craft knife and the combination square, go over the lines of the groove, marking across the faces and 10 mm down the sides. Also cut the line for the top of the bracket, marking both faces and both edges. These knife cuts will prevent the timber fibres from breaking out during cutting.

5 If you have a bench stop or hook, use it to support the material while you cut the grooves to the correct depth. If not, cramp your piece of material down to a surface suitable for cutting on. Cut the grooves, using the tenon saw, cutting on the waste side of the line so that the groove does not end up too wide. This is especially important when glass shelves are to be placed in the grooves, as they need to fit neatly for safety's sake.

6 Cramp the material to the work surface now if it is not already. Take up the 6 mm chisel and, with bevelled side up, line it up with the 10 mm mark on the edge of the material and strike the chisel with a

### GLASS SHELVES

• The thickness of glass necessary for these shelves depends on the length of the shelves. Up to a length of 600 mm the glass should be a minimum of 6 mm thick, between 600 mm and 1 m it should be 10 mm thick and between 1.0 and 1.2 m it should be 12 mm thick. If the shelf is over 1.2 m long you will need to insert a central support.

• It is best not to try to cut the glass, but to purchase the shelves already cut to size and shape, and with the edges smoothed.

hammer or mallet. Cut upwards towards the centre of the material. Turn the material around and repeat the process from the opposite edge. Continue to remove the waste material, levelling out the bottom of the groove as you go. Check for level by placing the edge of the chisel in the bottom of the groove and see if it rocks. If it does, more material may need to be removed from the

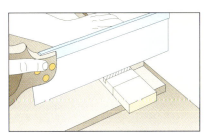

5 *Saw down the sides of the groove to a depth of 10 mm, sawing on the waste side of the line.*

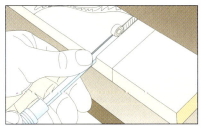

6 *Chisel out the waste from the groove, locating the chisel accurately and cutting upwards.*

*The glass shelves are firmly slotted into timber side brackets.*

centre of the groove until the chisel sits steady in the groove.

7 Check you have marked the pieces out in pairs. Use the jigsaw or coping saw to cut out the bracket shapes, working slowly and staying on the waste side of the lines. Keep the tool moving in a single cut and try to complete each bracket in one go. Trim the tops square with a jigsaw. Keep to the waste side of the line.

8 Match the brackets up in pairs (grooves and tops together) and check that the grooves line up and that the tops line up at the knife marks. Hold them together using masking tape. Place them in a vice and plane the tops flush and down to the knife lines. Avoid chipping out with the plane by using a backing block. (If you do not have a vice and plane, use a sanding block to sand out the jigsaw marks across the flat

## MAKING JOINTS

Joining timbers and board materials is a basic requirement when making shelves, and the most effective joints are rebates and housing joints. The quickest and most accurate way to make them is with a router but they can be made with specialised tools such as a rebate plane, or with a tenon or circular saw and chisel.

1 Mark out the positions of the joints on the timber. Continue the markings down the edges only as deep as the joint will be. Trace over the lines with a knife.

2 If using a circular saw, set the depth of the joint accurately on the saw, and cramp a batten across the board to guide the saw.

3 Saw across the face of the piece, on the waste side of the line.

4 Use the appropriate sized chisel to remove the waste until the bottom of the housing is flat and to the correct depth.

tops.) With the pieces still together, sand the curved edges with medium grade abrasive paper to get rid of the saw marks and then with fine grade paper to prepare the pieces for painting. Repeat this process with each pair. When working on the curved surfaces, use a short piece of

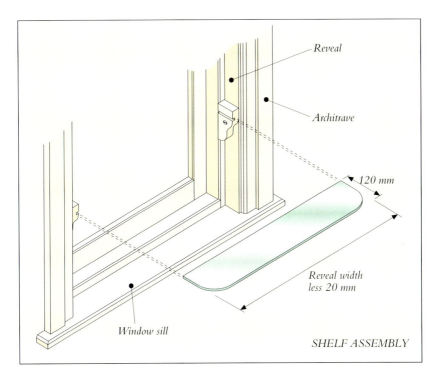

Reveal

Architrave

120 mm

Reveal width
less 20 mm

Window sill

SHELF ASSEMBLY

dowelling rod with abrasive paper wrapped around it.

## INSTALLATION

9 Use a spirit level to check the sill is level. Measure up from the sill, making allowance if it is not level, and locate the positions for the brackets on the reveal linings, as shown in the diagram above. Hold one bracket in position and fix it in with a 40 mm (1½ in) panel pin. Locate the matching bracket on the opposite side and fix it. Check with a spirit level that the two brackets are level and make any adjustments necessary. Fix the brackets to the reveal using 40 mm (1½ in) panel pins. If you prefer, the brackets can be fixed to the reveal linings with 40 mm (1½ in) screws and wall plugs (if necessary). Mark out the positions of the screw holes as indicated and drill them using a 5 mm drill bit while the brackets are still fastened together. Countersink the screw holes and fit the brackets.

10 Test the shelves for fit and adjust the groove depth if necessary. Remove the shelves and finish the brackets to match the reveal.

11 Place a very small amount of paintable silicone in the groove. This will keep the shelf in place if the fit is a little sloppy and prevent accidents. Slide in the shelves.

# Picture-rail shelf

This narrow shelf runs right around the room above the doors and windows, resting on a series of wooden brackets that can be shaped to match the style of the room.

MEASURING UP

1 Measure the room accurately to determine the length of timber required for the shelving and then calculate the number of brackets you will need. The brackets should be spaced no more than 1000 mm apart, and so first divide each wall length by 1000 and then go up to the next full number. Thus, if the wall is 3300 mm long, divide 3300 by 1000 to arrive at 3.33, or four brackets.

2 Locate bracket positions on the wall.
• For masonry walls, locate the first

and last brackets. The first bracket will be 250 mm away from the adjoining wall and the last will end 250 mm from the opposite wall. Deduct this 500 mm from the wall length: 3300 − 500 = 2800 mm. This is the space into which you will fit the other brackets. Then divide the 2800 mm by the number of spaces between the remaining brackets, that is, the number of brackets (two), plus one. In this example it is three spaces, so 2800 ÷ 3 = 933. The remaining brackets will, therefore, be spaced at 933 mm centres.

---

MATERIALS★

• 125 x 25 mm planed pine or other softwood (for brackets★★)

• 150 x 25 mm planed pine or other softwood (for the shelf)

• Small sheet of stiff cardboard for template

• Abrasive paper: two sheets of medium and one sheet of coarse

• 50 mm (2 in) x No.8 gauge countersunk wood screws (one per bracket)

• 40 mm (1½ in) x No.8 gauge countersunk wood screws (one per bracket)

• Construction adhesive for fixing brackets to wall

• Wall plugs or hollow wall anchors to suit

• Finish of choice

★ Finished width of shelf: 140 mm. Timber sizes given are nominal (see page 49).
★★ For each pair of brackets you will need 150 mm of 125 x 25 mm solid timber. See step 1 to determine how many you will need.

---

*The perfect way to display a collection of small objects, this easily-erected shelf also keeps them out of harm's way.*

## TOOLS

- Tape measure
- Compasses
- Combination square
- Scissors
- Pencil
- Cramp
- Jigsaw
- Sanding block
- Electric drill and drill stand
- Drill bits: 5 mm drill bit and countersink; 3 mm masonry bit
- Tenon saw or panel saw
- Orbital sander
- Straight-edge
- Spirit level
- Screwdriver (cross-head or slotted)

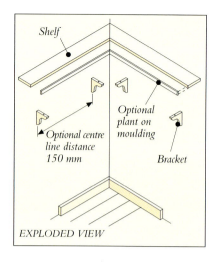

Shelf

Optional centre line distance 150 mm

Optional plant on moulding

Bracket

*EXPLODED VIEW*

• On timber-framed walls the spacing of the brackets is determined by the positions of the studs, and you need to determine the centre of each stud. Normally there is a stud at each end of the wall as the sheeting material is attached to it. This stud is generally 50 mm wide, so allowing for the sheeting material on the adjoining wall the centre of these studs should be about 15 mm away from the adjoining wall. Locate the intervening studs (see the box on page 62) and use a fine nail to penetrate the sheeting material to locate each stud centre precisely. Do this in an area that will be covered by the shelving to save making good later. (Note that there will be a stud on either side of each window and door to support the frames.) If the studs are close to 450 mm apart, you

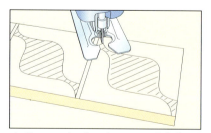

*4 Cramp the bracket material down to a suitable work surface and cut out the rough shape with a jigsaw.*

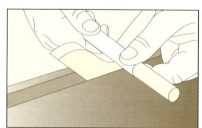

*5 To clean up the inside curves of the bracket, wrap a small piece of abrasive paper around a dowel rod.*

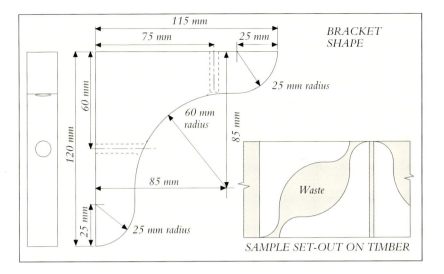

*BRACKET SHAPE*

*SAMPLE SET-OUT ON TIMBER*

will need to fix a bracket only at every second stud. As the shelving is not very heavy and will not be carrying a lot of weight, hollow wall anchors can also be used for fixing points where there is no stud.

## MAKING THE BRACKETS

3 Make a cardboard template of the bracket shape (see pattern above), using compasses and a combination square. Cut out the template and set it out on the bracket material. Transfer the pattern to the timber.

4 Cramp the bracket material to a suitable work surface and cut out the rough shape with a jigsaw. Be sure to wear safety glasses, keep the electric flex out of the way and always cut on the waste side of the line.

5 Clean up the surfaces. Without expensive machinery it is not easy to clean up curved surfaces cut with a jigsaw, but one way is to cramp several brackets together and use coarse grades of abrasive paper around a sanding block to remove the saw marks on the external curves. Then wrap a small piece of abrasive paper around a dowel rod and use it to smooth out the marks on the inside curves.

6 Make the screw holes. If you have one, use a drill stand with stops and a vice to keep the holes consistent.

---

HINT

When marking the shelf height around the room, it may be faster to use a water level and chalk line. This method can be carried out by one person, and it can often be more accurate than using a conventional spirit level.

---

Otherwise, keep the brackets cramped together and mark out the hole positions across all the brackets at the same time, using a combination square and pencil to get them in line. Using a drill with 5 mm bit, drill the holes as marked. Replace the bit with a countersink bit and countersink the holes.

## MAKING THE SHELVES

7 If you want the front edge of the shelf shaped, cut it with a router (remember to mitre the corners) or buy lengths of hardwood moulding from your local timber supplier and attach them, making allowances for them on the adjoining shelf lengths. Cut the shelves to their final length and mitre the ends that will fit together in the corners.

8 Having cut the shelves to length, hold them in position and check whether or not they fit neatly against the wall. The walls may be bowed one way or the other, which will leave unsightly gaps between the wall and the shelf. If the gaps are too large (more than 5 mm), you will need to

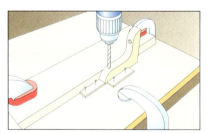

*6 Mark out the screw holes on the brackets and drill the holes. With a countersink bit countersink the holes.*

plane the boards to fit neatly against the wall.

## FINISHING AND INSTALLATION

9 When you are satisfied with the fit, take shelves and brackets and give a final sand. Finish as desired (see box on page 11).

10 Strike a level line around the room at the height at which the brackets will finish (you will probably need a friend to help). At one corner mark this height and raise a straight-edge to the position. Use the spirit level to check that the straight-edge is level and, with a pencil, mark a line on the wall.

11 Mark the centre line positions of the corner brackets and all the other brackets (see step 2). Take up the drill and appropriate drill bits and attach the brackets to the wall with the 50 mm (2 in) x No.8 gauge countersunk wood screws, placing a small drop of construction adhesive on the back of each before fixing them to the wall. Stretch a string line across the front edge of the brackets to see they all line up. Make the necessary adjustments to get them in line.

12 Lay the shelves on the brackets and secure them from below using 40 mm (1½ in) x No.8 gauge screws. A bit of construction adhesive on top of the brackets helps to hold the shelf in place. Fill gaps with a gap filler and touch up any marks on the finish.

# TIMBER

SOFTWOOD OR HARDWOOD?

Timber is classified as either softwood or hardwood, but this classification depends not on the relative hardness or density of the timber, but on the type of tree it comes from. For example, balsa, a softish timber used to make model aeroplanes and other lightweight models, is actually a hardwood. Hardwoods are mostly from deciduous trees that lose their leaves in winter; softwoods are from conifers with needle-like leaves.

For most of the projects in this book you can choose either a softwood or a hardwood. The main determining factors will be cost, availability and suitability for the particular project.

TIMBER CONDITIONS

Timber is sold in three conditions:
• sawn or rough sawn: brought to a specific (nominal) size by band saw
• planed, planed all round (PAR)
• moulded: processed to a specific profile for architraves, window sills, skirting boards and so on

Planed timber is sold using the same nominal dimensions as sawn timber, for example 100 x 50 mm, but the surfaces have all been machined down to a flat, even width and thickness so that the '100 x 50 mm' timber is actually between 95 x 45 mm and 97 x 47 mm. The chart below shows the sizes for planed timber sold in nominal sizes. Some suppliers now label wood with its 'actual' dimensions. Always check sizes before use.

Moulded timbers are also ordered by their nominal sizes. Their finished sizes will generally compare with those given in the chart for planed timber, but check them carefully at the timber yard as there will be many variations.

Timber is sold in standard lengths, beginning at 1.8 m and increasing by 300 mm to 2.1 m, 2.4 m and so on. Short lengths and off-cuts are also usually available.

| Sawn (nominal) size (mm) | Maximum size after planing (mm) |
| --- | --- |
| 10 | 7 |
| 12 | 9 |
| 19 | 16 |
| 25 | 22 |
| 32 | 29 |
| 38 | 35 |
| 50 | 47 |
| 75 | 72 |
| 100 | 97 |
| 125 | 122 |
| 150 | 147 |
| 175 | 172 |
| 200 | 197 |
| 225 | 222 |
| 250 | 247 |
| 300 | 297 |

*A gateleg shelf or table provides a useful extra surface but folds out of the way when it is no longer needed.*

# Gateleg shelf

This shelf doubles as a small table and is supported on a gateleg bracket so that it folds down out of the way when not in use. The elliptical shape is not difficult to achieve.

## DRAWING THE PATTERN
1 Draw out the components on the MDF sheet (see the cutting pattern on page 53). We used a sheet 1200 x 600 mm; if your sheet is a different size, adjust the layout. Using the combination square mark out the shelf strip (800 x 300 mm) along one long edge of the sheet. Then mark another line, parallel to the first to allow for the saw thickness. Mark the centre, point A, on the inner line. This will serve as the x-axis for the semi-elliptical shelf (see the diagram on page 52).

## MATERIALS★

| PART | MATERIAL | LENGTH | WIDTH | NO. |
|------|----------|--------|-------|-----|
| Back board | 18 mm MDF | 800 mm | 245 mm | 1 |
| Drop shelf | 18 mm MDF | 800 mm | 320 mm | 1 |
| Shelf strip | 18 mm MDF | 800 mm | 30 mm | 1 |
| Gateleg bracket | 18 mm MDF | 300 mm | 190 mm | 1 |

OTHER: Three 25 mm (1 in) panel pins; one piano hinge 900 mm long; thirty 15 mm (⅝ in) x No.5 gauge countersunk screws (cross-head or slotted); five 40 mm (1½ in) x No.8 gauge countersunk screws (cross-head or slotted); masking tape; wall fixings (see step 11); PVA adhesive; finish of choice

★ Maximum width of the shelf is 368 mm, length 800 mm. For a note on MDF see page 25.

## TOOLS

- Combination square
- Tape measure
- Pencil
- String
- Hammer
- Straight-edge
- Safety glasses
- Dust mask
- Jigsaw
- Circular saw
- Plane
- Flat-bottomed spoke-shave (optional)
- Orbital sander (optional)
- Hacksaw
- Smooth cut file
- Electric drill
- Drill bits: 5 mm, 2 mm
- Countersink bit
- Medium paint brush
- Screwdriver
- Two G-cramps

2 Draw in the y-axis through point A, at right angles to the x-axis, drawing the line right across the board to the opposite edge. Measure 320 mm along it from A and mark point Y. Place the end of the tape measure at Y and move it along the x-axis to locate the two points B so that each line Y–B is 400 mm long. Place the panel pins at both B points and Y, pushing them in slightly, just

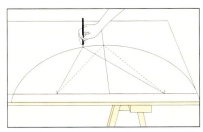

*2 Mark out the triangle base for the semi-elliptical shape, and then use a pencil and string to draw the shape.*

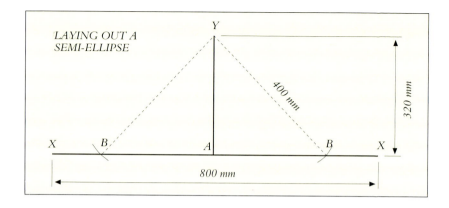

**LAYING OUT A SEMI-ELLIPSE**

Y

400 mm

320 mm

X          B          A          B          X

800 mm

enough to take a little tension. Tie the string to one B point, pull it past the Y point and tie it to the other B point. Now replace the Y pin with a pencil and draw the half-ellipse, remembering to keep the string taut.

3 Mark out the back board as shown on the cutting pattern, placing the apex at the centre line. The gateleg bracket can be set out across a corner to eliminate a couple of saw cuts.

## CUTTING OUT
4 Use a G-cramp to hold the material to the work surface. Put on your safety glasses and dust mask and,

using your jigsaw, carefully cut out the elliptical shape, including the shelf strip. It will be cut off at a later stage. Remember to keep to the waste side of the line.

5 Cut off the shelf strip and cut out the remaining components with the circular saw. Clean up all the straight edges with the smoothing plane or, if you do not have a plane, give them a good sanding with an orbital sander to remove any unsightly saw marks— they would show up clearly under the paint. Do not sand the face surfaces of MDF, as this makes the finish furry. If the surface is marked,

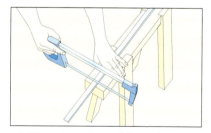

*5 Use a circular saw to cut out the back board. A straight edge cramped to the board acts as a guide.*

*6 Cut the piano hinge into two pieces, one 180 mm long for the gateleg bracket and one for the shelf.*

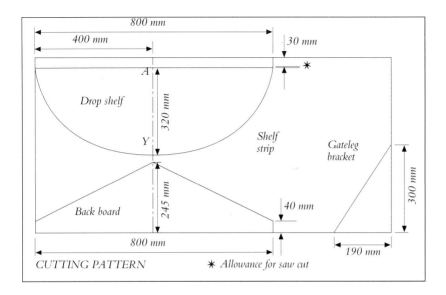

CUTTING PATTERN    * Allowance for saw cut

use a wood filler and sand lightly with fine grade abrasive paper. Clean up the elliptical shelf with a flat-bottomed spokeshave, the plane or by careful hand sanding.

6 Using the hacksaw, cut 180 mm off the 900 mm length of piano hinge. This will be used for the gateleg flap, the remainder being for the drop shelf. File the ends of the hinge to remove sharp edges.

ASSEMBLY

7 Align the shelf and shelf strip, leaving a 1–2 mm gap between them (a piece of cardboard is about the right width). Open out the piano hinge and centre it on the joint line. Use a 2 mm bit in your drill to provide a starting or pilot hole for the 15 mm (⅝ in) x No.5 gauge screws. A piece of masking tape will

help hold the hinge in position while you are lining up the first few screws.

8 Mark out the position of the shelf on the back board. Locate the positions for the five 40 mm (1½ in) x No.8 gauge screws, as shown on the exploded view on page 54. Then drill 5 mm clearance holes and countersink the back. Align the shelf on the back board and drill 3 mm pilot holes into the shelf strip. Apply adhesive to the edges with the paint brush, realign the parts and fasten the screws securely home.

9 Attach the short piece of piano hinge to the short edge of the bracket, as described in step 7. You may need to drill the hinge and add two more screws near the top of the hinge for strength, being careful not to split the board. Open out the

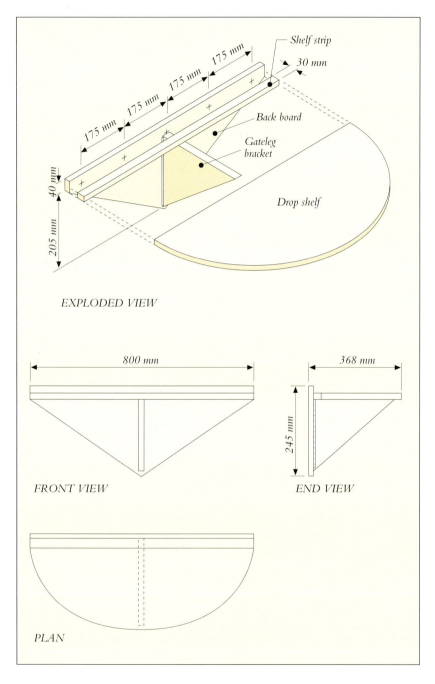

Shelf strip

30 mm

175 mm 175 mm 175 mm 175 mm 175 mm 175 mm

Back board

Gateleg bracket

Drop shelf

40 mm

205 mm

EXPLODED VIEW

800 mm

FRONT VIEW

368 mm

245 mm

END VIEW

PLAN

hinge and align the bracket with the centre line of the back board. Make sure the bracket will not foul on other parts of the shelf, and then fix it to the back board.

## FINISHING AND INSTALLATION

10 Remove the hinges and apply your finish of choice (see the box on page 11).

11 While the paint is drying, prepare the materials and tools used for installation. First determine whether you have a masonry wall or a hollow wall as this will determine what type of tools and fasteners will be needed. For masonry walls use 75 mm (3 in) nylon anchors, 75 mm (3 in) x No.10 gauge countersunk screws with appropriate plastic wall plugs or 75 mm (3 in) countersunk frame fixers. For framed walls use 75 mm (3 in) x No.10 gauge countersunk wood screws. Then, using a spirit level, draw a level line 730 mm above the floor. The shelf, when open, should sit level with this.

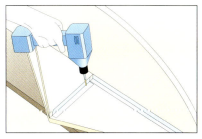

*9 Attach the hinge to the bracket, drilling two holes near the top for the extra screws, and to the back board.*

*The elliptical shape of the shelf ensures it will still be an attractive feature when it is folded away.*

12 If you have a timber-framed or stud partition wall you will need to locate the centres of the studs (see the box on page 62). Note the distance between studs and carefully transfer the positions to the back board. Make sure the fasteners are located below the shelf. Drill the back board of the shelf. With masonry walls just drill the two holes below the shelf line big enough for the chosen fasteners to pass through.

13 Hold the fixture up to the wall, making sure it is aligned with the level line previously struck, and drill the hole for the first fastener. Secure the fastener and check the level. When you are satisfied it is level, drill and secure the second fastener. Applying a little construction adhesive to the back board before fastening the shelf unit to the wall will improve the holding power.

# Free-standing shelf unit

Recycled fence palings or other softwood slats are used to make this shelf unit but any timber would serve as well. The shelves are made independently and bolted to the slats.

## PREPARING THE TIMBER

1 Lay out the slats. If using palings remove the nails and select the best ones, that is, the straightest ones with a uniform thickness. You will need about thirty-five slats altogether.

2 Take the framing material and mark off and cut the lengths required. Mark across the face and down the edges with the square and pencil to ensure that you have a squared line to follow when cutting. Always cut on the waste side of the pencil line. Hold the combination square against the timber to provide a guide for the saw to run against. If you are not completely proficient

| MATERIALS** | | | |
|---|---|---|---|
| PART | MATERIAL | LENGTH | NO. |
| Side/back slats | old fence palings or 100 x 12 mm softwood★ | 1500 mm | 16 |
| Shelf slats | old fence palings or 100 x 12 mm softwood★ | 776 mm★★★ | 16 |
| Frame stiles | 50 x 25 mm rough-sawn softwood | 776 mm★★★ | 8 |
| Frame rails | 50 x 25 mm rough-sawn softwood | 335 mm★★★ | 12 |
| Plinth rails | 50 x 25 mm rough-sawn softwood | 298 mm | 4 |
| Plinth face | old fence paling or 100 x 12 mm softwood★ | 776 mm★ | 1 |

OTHER: Abrasive paper: coarse and fine; PVA adhesive; 60 mm (2½ in) lost-head nails; 30 mm (1¼ in) wire nails; four plastic scouring pads; clean rags; Danish teak oil or finish of choice; eighty-four 50 x 6 mm (2 x ¼ in) bolts, nuts and washers.

★ For slat material see the box on page 58.
★★ Finished height of unit 1500 mm; width 795 mm; shelf depth 378 mm. Timber sizes given are nominal. For timber types and sizes, see page 49.
★★★ Sizes depend on actual timber sizes.

*This attractive shelf unit is a perfect way to re-use palings or other old timber. Slats are nailed to the shelf frames as well as providing the side and back timber, and the whole is finished with teak oil.*

## TOOLS

- Hammer
- Combination square
- Measuring tape
- Pencil
- Hand saw or circular saw
- Safety goggles
- Gloves
- Dust mask
- Mitre saw or tenon saw and mitre box
- Bench hook
- Orbital sander
- Smoothing plane
- Electric drill
- Drill bit: 6.5 mm
- Wire brush for electric drill
- Four G-cramps
- 11 mm socket and socket wrench

## SLATS

We used old fence palings in this unit but it will look just as effective if made using strips of 100 x 12 mm softwood.

If you are using old palings, you will need at least thirty-five for the best results, so that you can choose those that are straight and of a consistent thickness. Old palings are well seasoned and should remain dimensionally stable. You may need, however, to adjust the width and depth of the unit to suit the particular palings you have.

with a circular saw, use a mitre saw or tenon saw and bench hook.

3 Stack two or three slats on top of each other and square them off near one end. When they all are cut square at one end, mark and cut them to 1500 mm in length. Trim the tops with angled cuts as shown in the diagram. There is no need to be too fussy with the angle and size as a slight unevenness will add to the rustic appeal.

4 Cut the shelf slats, using the technique described in step 2.

5 Using coarse abrasive paper, sand all the components to remove any splintering timber. Plane the top edges only of the frame material to give a clean, straight edge (this will make it easier to glue on the slats). Plane a light 2 mm chamfer on the edges of the frame members.

## ASSEMBLING THE FRAMES

6 Take a frame rail and place it in the vice with one end facing up. Spread a little PVA adhesive on the

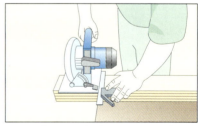

*3 Stack several slats on top of each other and square them off near one end. Cut them to length.*

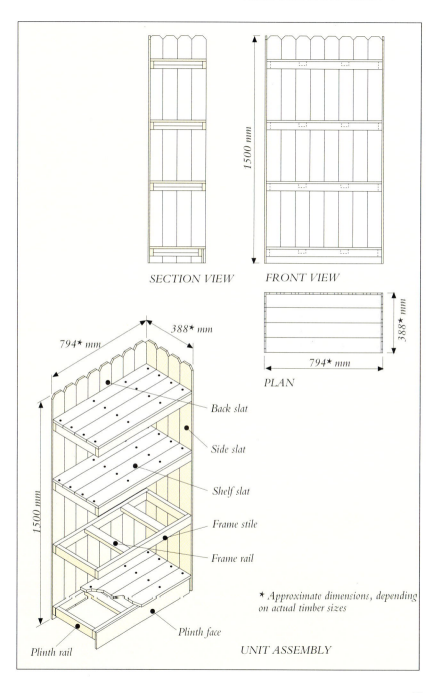

SECTION VIEW

FRONT VIEW

1500 mm

388* mm

794* mm

PLAN

388* mm

794* mm

Back slat

Side slat

Shelf slat

Frame stile

Frame rail

Plinth face

Plinth rail

1500 mm

388* mm

794* mm

* Approximate dimensions, depending
on actual timber sizes

UNIT ASSEMBLY

59

end grain and rub it in with your finger. Then place another small amount of adhesive on the end of the timber. This ensures good penetration and a stronger joint. Take a stile and start a 50 mm (2 in) nail into the face of the timber, near the end. Locate the stile on the rail so that the ends are flush and the planed edges are aligned accurately. Hammer in the nail and adjust the fit. Hammer a second nail into the joint and then repeat this process for the other end. Check that the frames are square by measuring the diagonal distance across the frames from corner to corner. When these measurements are the same, the frame is square.

7 Add the mid-rails to the frame. They should be spaced evenly but the exact position is not essential as long as the faces are flush with the top of the frame stiles.

8 Construct two more shelf frames and the plinth frame, which uses the shorter rails.

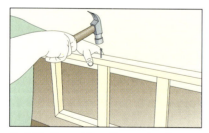

*7 Add the mid-rails to the frame, spacing them evenly and making sure they are flush with the top.*

## ASSEMBLING THE SHELVES

9 While the adhesive is drying on the frames, scrub and sand the slats if necessary. Wear safety goggles and gloves, and if possible use a wire brush fitted to an electric drill to scrub all along each slat, both sides and edges, paying attention to the areas where most rot and decay have occurred. A plain wire brush can be used but the process will be more laborious and take longer. When all slats have been wire brushed, sand them using coarse abrasive paper. Be sure to sand the edges well to remove splinters and sand along the grain, not across it. For a smooth finish go over each piece again using medium abrasive paper. Brush off the sanding dust with a soft brush.

10 Check the adhesive is dry. Take the plinth frame (it is narrower), and using PVA adhesive and the 30 mm (1¼ in) wire nails, nail on the front plinth, making sure the top edge is flush with the top of the frame.

11 Apply a generous quantity of adhesive to the area on the plinth frame where the front slat is to be fixed and lay the slat on the frame so that it overhangs the plinth facing by no more than 10 mm. Check that it is flush with or just slightly over the end of the frame and nail it on with lost-head nails. Apply some more adhesive to the frame, position the next slat and nail it on, ensuring that the ends line up. Repeat this process for a third slat. Leave the fourth slat

*The angled cuts on top of the slats look more rustic if a little irregular.*

for now: it will be too wide to fit and will have to be cut down to size.

12 Fix three slats to each of the shelf frames in the same way, setting them flush with the front face of the frame.

13 Place the fourth slats in position on the frames and mark the necessary width right along their length. Cramp them to a suitable work surface and saw or plane them to width. Nail the final slats in position.

## PREPARING THE SIDE AND BACK SLATS

14 Take one side slat and measure 60 mm up from the bottom. From this mark measure a further three 400 mm increments for the positions of the other shelves. Mark a line down the centre of the slat to locate the four positions for drilling the holes. Place a 6.5 mm drill bit in the drill and drill these positions.

15 Use the first slat as a template for drilling the remaining slats. Stack two or three slats together with the template on top. Cramp them together and drill right through the stack at the appropriate positions.

16 Apply the finish to all the side slats and shelves (access to these surfaces will be difficult later). We used Danish teak oil to give a rustic appearance as it makes the grain stand out. Rub it well into the grain of the timber using fine wire wool and a circular motion. This will pick up any small splinters that the sanding missed, so wear appropriate gloves. Use a dry, clean cloth to wipe off all the excess oil. The bolt heads were painted matt black. They were pushed through a sheet of corrugated cardboard, leaving only the heads exposed, and spray painted.

## ASSEMBLY

17 Clear a space for assembly. You may need another pair of hands at this stage. Take the base shelf and stand it on its end. Take the first side

slat and position it so it is flush with the bottom edge of the plinth and the front edge of the shelf slat. Use a cramp to hold it in position. Take the remaining shelves and cramp them flush with the edge of the slat in their correct positions, making sure the bolts will go through the middle of the shelf frames and there is clearance for a socket spanner. Drill the holes in the frames—the bolt holes into the plinth will have to be angled back a little to clear the framework but this will not affect the final appearance. Place 50 x 6 mm (2 x ¼ in) bolts into the holes, add the washers and nuts and do them up, finger tight only at this stage.

18 Take the next slat and line it up with the bottom of the first slat. Using a combination square laying along the front edge, check the new slat is square to the last slat and the plinth is sitting square to the front edge of the first slat. Repeat the squaring check at each shelf position and cramp the pieces in place. Drill the holes and place bolts into them. Repeat this for the other two slats. Do not trim off the overhang. Tighten up the bolts.

19 Place down a groundsheet and turn the unit over. Place the first slat on the other side, flush with the plinth and shelves as described in step 11. Check that the distance between the shelves is the same on both sides and cramp the slat into position. Drill the holes and insert the bolts. Fix the other slats to the side.

## FINDING STUDS IN A FRAME OR STUD PARTITION WALL

In order to fix a shelf to a timber frame or stud partition wall, you will need to locate the studs. This can be done in several ways.
• Use a stud finder (joist and batten detector). This is a battery operated instrument designed to locate studs. It is available from most DIY stores.
• Tap gently on the wall and listen for the solid sound.
• Use a bradawl at shelf height to locate the studs.
• Look for nail marks in the plaster work as they may indicate the stud positions.
• Climb into the roof cavity and find the tops of the studs. Then measure their distance apart and the distance from the corner.

20 Lay the unit on its face and add the back slats. Work from both sides to the centre, so that if the palings do not fit evenly, the two centre ones can be trimmed down to fit. This looks better than having a narrow paling at one end. Drill the bolt holes, angling them towards the bottom of the unit to avoid bolts fouling slightly on the framing members. Insert the bolts. Stand the unit up, place the washers and nuts on the bolts and tighten the bolts.

21 A second application of teak oil can now be made.

# Tools for making shelves

Some of the most useful tools for making shelves are shown below. Build up your tool kit gradually—most of the tools can be purchased from your local hardware store.

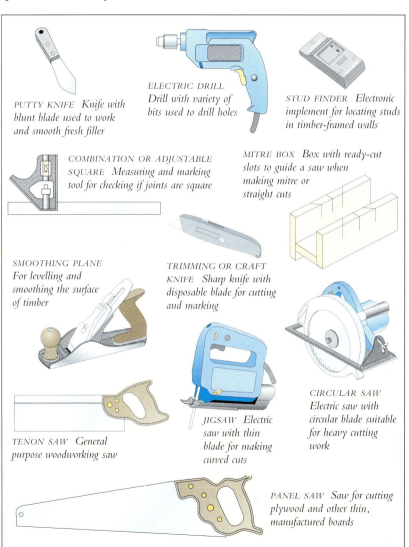

PUTTY KNIFE  *Knife with blunt blade used to work and smooth fresh filler*

ELECTRIC DRILL *Drill with variety of bits used to drill holes*

STUD FINDER  *Electronic implement for locating studs in timber-framed walls*

COMBINATION OR ADJUSTABLE SQUARE  *Measuring and marking tool for checking if joints are square*

MITRE BOX  *Box with ready-cut slots to guide a saw when making mitre or straight cuts*

SMOOTHING PLANE *For levelling and smoothing the surface of timber*

TRIMMING OR CRAFT KNIFE  *Sharp knife with disposable blade for cutting and marking*

CIRCULAR SAW *Electric saw with circular blade suitable for heavy cutting work*

TENON SAW  *General purpose woodworking saw*

JIGSAW  *Electric saw with thin blade for making curved cuts*

PANEL SAW  *Saw for cutting plywood and other thin, manufactured boards*

# Index